A BEND IN THE ROAD

A BEND IN THE ROAD

POEMS BY

EAMON J. MCENEANEY

CORNELL UNIVERSITY LIBRARY

© 2004 Bonnie McEneaney

All rights reserved. No part of this publication may be reproduced or transmitted in any form or by any means, electronic or mechanical, including photocopying, recording, or by any information storage and retrieval system, without written permission from the publisher.

Published by Cornell University Library, Ithaca, New York 14853.

ISBN 0-935995-04-8

Jacket and text design by Lou Robinson

Library of Congress Control Number: 2004113156

To all the people who tragically lost their lives
on September 11, 2001,
and to the families they left behind—especially
Brendan, Jennifer, Kyle, and Kevin

Words,
rebellious tools at times!

CONTENTS

ACKNOWLEDGMENTS

With thanks to all the people at Cornell University who gave their time and effort to bringing this project to fruition— Ken McClane, Sarah Thomas, Elaine Engst, Eleanor Brown, Marisue Taube, Kenneth Williams, C.J. Lance, and Kari Smith—and special thanks to John Gilbert, who with complete dedication pulled the team together on this project and built the foundation. John, we are forever grateful.

FOREWORD

When you touch a book, you touch a man, and this is certainly true in this powerful collection of Eamon McEneaney's lyrics. These poems are wide-ranging and passionate: there are love lyrics, elegies, and celebrations of the occasional. And, most importantly, these poems are bighearted, full of trenchancy and life. Like Yeats, McEneaney imagines the world awash in splendor, politics, and announcements; like Yeats, McEneaney knows that the mythic is tied to history and the heart. The mind may teach us things, but it is the heart that brings us into communion with the world, with the seen and the need-to-be seen.

In Eamon's world, to be bighearted is to be truthful: to comprehend that "If I love then I be good," but "If I despise then I but kindle wood for Hell's fire." For Eamon, the world is "a sweet renaissance—a season of spring." But then, just as truthfully, he reminds us, as if listening to the hidden gyres, "I fear the winds bring winter, and other sorrowful things."

Other poems, of course, are playful. There's a hip-hop insouciance in some of them, and one can rejoice in the lovely windswept hair of a child on a beach, conspire with the intemperate "facedom" demanded on the I.R.T., and be awed by his love for his wife, Bonnie, which is ineluctable, powerful, and deep. But always after a delicious respite, the human rejoinder:

I grow without the aid
of another beside me
and converse with loneliness—
We speak in two angled fork tongue—
We try, but fail to fool one another—
because there is little to nothing,
or nothing too little to say…

These poems are bighearted; they are maps of a big
spirit, a wondrous, probing, luminescent soul. Sadly, I
did not know Eamon McEneaney personally, but I do
know him. The generosity of these poems makes me
understand the generosity of his friends, for Eamon's
great work was his ability to "inspirit." As one of his
friends said, "I thought of myself merely as a jock and
he had me reading poetry." Well, this is what poetry can
do: it can transform the preconceived.

When you touch a book, you touch a man. What a
miracle this collection is! And how lucky we are to have
a heart so full that it turns us all to wonder.

I was told the rain would stop
and it has not!
I was told to watch for stars
in the east
and they have not come—
I kicked an empty can
across the world,
it made no noise;
birds in the branches
lost song,

all about darkness grew
the wind died
and so I sang to myself.

Although we no longer have Eamon in the flesh,
which is a tragedy beyond language and all understanding, thank goodness we have his heart's music. Listen:

the ground loosens with each new day
& with each new day,
new signs of spring come,
returning—
like the lily & the cypress & the sparrow.

Kenneth A. McClane
W. E. B. DuBois Professor of Literature
Cornell University

INTRODUCTION

*M*ost people think of Eamon McEneaney as an extremely gifted athlete. After all, he was inducted into the U.S. Lacrosse Hall of Fame, the Cornell University Hall of Fame, and the Long Island Lacrosse Hall of Fame. For three years in a row, he was First Team All American in Lacrosse, and in 1977 he was NCAA Lacrosse Player of the Year. He shares the world record for points in a lacrosse championship series (*Guinness Book of World Records 1997*), he was All Ivy in football, and he excelled in golf, tennis, and squash.

One can understand how younger lacrosse players emulated him, how his opponents on the field respected him. Some of the letters I've received talk of how entire opposing teams would review tapes of his plays after games—frequently asking each other, "How did he do that?"

Eamon was a talented athlete, but I like to think of him as a gifted writer, crafting wonderful short stories and poems. This was a side to him that most people did not know. He could weave words into images evoking the deepest emotions from the reader. He was a passionate writer. He created works of art, like paint on a canvas, for us to ponder—some incredibly beautiful, some disturbing. He wrote about how he saw the world and the things that were most important to him. And he warned us of devastating consequences if we didn't have the right priorities in life. One poem, in particular—"Madhattan"—hits home.

On September 11, 2001, Eamon died in the North Tower of the World Trade Center. Although published posthumously, this book of poetry brings to reality one of the dreams he had—to publish his poems so that they could be shared with others, and be a frame of reference for reflection. His poetry serves as a reminder of the fragility of life, that each day we are given is a precious gift—this should never be forgotten.

Bonnie McEneaney

PREFACE

my poems are written to be shared,
for myself
and whoever may come
to the road in which they lay:
take them as you may.

i cannot tell you right from wrong
for these answers can only
be found within.
i cannot show you truth
from the nonsensical thoughts
that surround this world.
no man has benefited
by cheating another one:
this I know, myself, to be true.

in my poet's eyes i see truth,
and try to live by its light.
true brotherhood is only felt
by the warmth this light
brings to the heart.

e. j. m.

LIFE

The wind

The wind blows time across America's
golden cornfields.
Time and clouds drift
bringing the storm.
Blue and white mixing gray for the skyline
that lies tired above
for now.

With each breath
Another dimension unfolds.
Like waves of the sea
The universe unfolds,
Becoming calm
becoming the womb.

Lay down your aging robes,
leave them for another,
travel to another dimension,
for new dreams to uncover.

The wind blows wild through our skeleton lives.
For what will ever become of the cornfields and
storm skylines
and us,
after the wind passes?
What will become of the tired universe after the wind
blows her away?

The rainbows are black and white
Pushing the wind back into the night
Blonde and young
So much fun
The golden age soon to be done
The wind blows new seeds into existence.

We haven't the time

It has been a short life
        once again
Yellowish and Red
        the trees soon to be resting again

Tears of time
What a false conception
There is no time
There is only living and dying
Happiness and crying

Fall teaches us life and all its values.
Traveling through the timeless terrain
all the time our eyes to be wide
our ears to be spying
        on the external and internal existence

Deep penetration into the sad child's head.
        Let him sleep!
I have seen enough tears to drown an eternity of days.
        Please let him sleep.
Let ghost tales race around his feather-light head.
Fairy godmothers snatch his baby tooth and leave but
a precious dream.

Where has imagery gone,
            no one knows,
No time left for things to be left undone.
Time ticks & ticks,
The age of compacted lives,
Let's not walk down the path of life,
            let's drive.

Tears fall down the young child's cheek,
            unable to understand,
Why life passes,
A flower never to melt in his appreciative hand.
We haven't the time, me boy,
            haven't the time to spend on such nonsense.

You must prepare for tomorrow,
            remember there is always tomorrow.
But father, I look at the wonders and realize
            I haven't the time
                in one life's span
To catch such beauty & hold it forever in my empty hand.
            Father, are you listening?

Aging

We ran so far in a galaxy of fun
But it's over now
It's over
It's done

In the corner
The dog lies
The babies cry—
The people die—
The old women in tired black dresses
Bow their heads for living.

In a smile
The world turns
A tear in time
The sun burns

The dreams
Yes the dreams
How we love when we dream!

Walking trails

While walking today
A voice arrived—
Loud and solid with truth—

Life's a challenge.
Fight it and feel her heart beat as
It screams with joy.

Kiss her breast
And feel the warmth and the softness
Like ice cream in summer.

Accept its receding hairline
And the wrinkles that surround her eyes
After this;
        Death is just another sunset
                in winter—

Coward?

I am going on a starvation existence
    fluids that is the existent,
I want to put myself to the test,
I want to meet myself at the
    threshold of death,
And shake hands with her eye to eye,
    I await the confrontation.
Ended 48 hours,
    coward?

Salmon

We Are Only But The Salmon
In The Stream,
Fighting The Currents Of Life
So That We May Provide Only
The Initial Breath For Our
Offspring—

Directionless

Each generation
with its own perspective
on life
wanders directionless down
the ancient road of time.
Youth with a golden circus
of curls
runs reckless and inconsiderate
into the older,
more knowledgeable.

There's something inside me

I.
There's something inside me
that weathers me each day
and each day it comes
black and thick
like cloud-burst.

When will the sun
rise in the west?
When will the star glass
snow on the sea?

II.
Having watched
the millions pass, and
being not first
nor neither last
I find transition through
the funnel
of an hourglass

There's something inside me
that weathers me each day,
and like the minute,
the moment, the death;
each leads into another—
until we're at rest.

The irony

Oh! the irony of it all!
with our eyes fixed in
the front of our heads,
we walk forward into the future,
seeing only the days
we left behind.

Untitled

Listening to the radio late at night
there was this cat,
screaming, "Who will save our planet?
Who will save our world?"
Lying down I thought,
Who will save our planet from what?
The only thing we must save
our planet from,
is ourselves!

Who stops to listen?

Emptiness of trains running north to nowhere,
        razors splitting the brain into
                pieces of suicide soup,
The body crashing rocks that lie underneath the walk
bridges
& the world spins us all into a corner at one time or
another
Where to run,
When to see,
As the laughter of the human race echoes,
                &
                echoes,
                until the end.

Know one,
        Know them all,
They never stop to hear the bells toll
Angel Wings flap vigorously,
Trying desperately to catch the young boy's confusion
        Who stops to listen?

        Caring becoming virtue,
and the fatal rocks lie waiting patiently for its victim
        step
                by
                        step
                                up & over
                                        SPLAT

Another victim lost in the parade.
And the human race keeps marching,
never to step in the way of progression.

The dreamer

The skyline of my mind is filled with clouds.

I,

    uncertain of my thoughts sit in
    comfortable frustration for tomorrow.

I,

    waiting for the knock upon the
    crickety old door am deaf.

I,

    searching for the yellow rays of sunlight
    to squeeze between the walls of my brain am blind.

I,

    crying into the cup of yesterday,
    leaning on the doors of tomorrow,
    frightened by the stars that shine
    truth into my naked eyes,
        am a dreamer.

Sometimes

Sometimes,
    Age makes us unable to wear a smile.
    Words are flocked together for the
    Sake of conversation; and nature
    With her cool breezes and songbirds
    Singing is practical truth,
        crystallized
           and beautiful.

Sometimes,
    I hear the thoughts of man.
    Potential supermen await the cry.
    But I know that man is but the
    Insect of the Universe,
    The only potential is the uncovered
    Soil in which he lays

Sometimes,
    I grow lonely.
    For nothingness nourishes upon my soul.
    Like the autumn leaves that sway
    And fall, loneliness is only present,
    Until we reach the ground.

Neutron bomb

the ground loosens with each new day
& with each new day,
new signs of spring come,
returning —
like the lily & the cypress & the sparrow

all winter long
I've sat & contemplated
watched & walked
trudged & labored
in the snow covered fields
of thought & situation

all winter long
through the slush of silent, frozen madness
I dreamt of my youth
I dreamt of its paranoia
I remembered my dreams of the door
the walls of the school
the black desolated haze of the room

I remembered the air-raid drills
& the planes overhead
the times we hid in the cellar
like rats eyeing daylight,
away from the windows
frightened by something far greater
than any sun

I remembered people
like automated insects;
both in motion & mentality,
running to newly installed
fall-out shelters
practicing—
anticipating the final football

I couldn't help but feel then
as I feel now,
in my sullen skeleton weakness
how it is the world's madness;
is not my own

now
spring winks into being

all winter long
I've heard the blast & crackling
of this neutron bomb
seen its clouds of contamination
engulf advancing Russian tanks

watched a war build in my imagination
& fall ill in the eyes of our creator

then
            SUDDENLY!!!

sacred spring silently exuberantly shouted!!!

let it be
for you are as helpless,
as a winter turned spring

enjoy the beauty & wonder
that life does bring

Eating prunes in the big apple

the silver Rolls Royce with mag wheels
& chrome dashboard, bar, tv &
stereo…wasn't mine…

the greasy-grimy-hobo-drunken-
sailor-bum—with a neck that
hadn't been washed in weeks
wasn't crippled after all…
but rather dead.
& why didn't I stop to ask him
why on 5th & 45th & it the
4th of July?
I was busy!
& so I was…walking down
5th avenue…
watching the strange armies
of facedom
pass me by…

Gossip columns

hey,
heard you made the gossip column,
today.
good show.
bet you're gonna make a lot
of dough,
you're not just another schmo,
today.

hey,
you're gonna be known in
all the bars,
and all those people,
and all those eyes,
are gonna know your name,
check you out in freeze-frame
as you make your way
to the washroom
to clean yourself off
or powder yourself
with blank importance.

get with it, man,
crazyhorse would never
be photographed
and gossip columns
never held up anything.

When glass onions break

down the block
a six sewer cap homer
from needle park
lurking in the filth and dark
Judas waits for infamy
and like a kiss
he gets an autograph
now the deed must be done.

eyes I dare not meet
in nightmare,
knees squatting in the shadows
the way a rabid dog urinates,
he squats...

a limousine pulls up
a gun is drawn
and then the shots
over at the Dakota
media people mingled
talked shop, why not?
they had discovered the genius,

created the hype
converged on the boys
with cameras and mikes,
blew them up like balloons
bigger than life,

behaving the way children behave,
never wanting to let the string go,
even after john was gone.
his imagination
shining on; new worlds to grow.

Darkness to light

To wish upon a falling star
on all the days that aren't
and are used.

To take the steps from
darkness to light
from shadows to fulfillment.

To have faith in the circle
full, unbroken,
infinite, destined
in her will—

There's no zen about it

there's no zen about it
that's what it is,

take it from someone
that's been in the biz,

there's no zen about it
that's the quiz,

that's the quiz,
believe me, it is.

the "cat in the hat"
hadn't a clue,
he was just doin'
what he was doin'
and comin' through...

there's no zen about it
just a balancing act,

a beachball, a
ten pin, 15 pies
and a hat.

SPIRITUALITY

God's heart

The sun
God's heart
shone on me.
Bright and clean with love
it gleamed,
as I ran
      free.

Soul

When we are able to place
ourselves inside the wings
of the butterfly and feel its
fluid motion,

When we are able to enter the
head of the ant and see through
its eyes; and to feel the
burden of the bread that
lies upon its back:

This is the time when we are
enlightened
and only begin to
touch upon the borders
of the eternal spirit
the borders of the soul.

Prayer of redemption

to multiply fish and loaves
and be my brother,
to spindle rags to clothes
for someone other.

I'm picking up
O'Casey's knife
Gathering giveness
Dispersing light

I'm pulling the
bloody thorns
from his brow,
perhaps in love
he'll receive me now?

I sang to myself

I was told the rain would stop
and it has not!
I was told to watch for stars
in the east
and they have not come—
I kicked an empty can
across the world,
it made no noise;
birds in the branches
lost song,
all about darkness grew
the wind died
and so I sang to myself.

Experiment i

i
a rat
encaged
my creator
watches
me behave
if
i
love
then
i
be good
if
i
despise
then
i
but kindle wood
for hell's fire.

Letter to a friend after his father's passing

It is sad this world of ours,
And loved ones like days seem to pass. Tears?
They make our eyes red, they make our hearts
step down to our stomachs.
They make us grow.

Old comrade,
dear friend, we too shall depart.
On an old beat up road that men walk and children
dance down, we met. The wave of the hand that
greeted us shall wave much louder on our departure day.

Hearts that crossed,
separate to be lost, but not forgotten.
Yes, and on this day when the trees are hanging sad
signs of Winter's hello, and Autumn's good-bye,
we still must travel on.

When the sky of gray lays on top of us and we feel
we can no longer breathe, try to remember she too
must depart, she too must leave, so we can feel free
again.

Sometimes I want to crawl away,
leave this sad bus for a day. But the day of this
shall soon arrive.

The trouble with love is that we think
of it too much in the physical sense. The
true light of love sits on her throne in the spirit,
facing change each day.
The spirit lurks in all things:
  the future,
  the memory,
all things essential to life.

  Don't carry the weight—
remember Jesus fell with the cross.
Carry your heart,
and the hearts of your brothers.
The sun shines you'll see.

Love is not past,
  nor present,
  nor now,
love is timeless.

When I live my next life I promise to love you,
  always.

A gift of tears to William Butler Yeats

The streets are filled by a crier's voice,
inside my window my thoughts are not of today.
I look though my tears which are cold and moist,
and dream of you, who have skipped away.

Silly hills of laughter where you and Maude danced,
her dress made of wind that drifted to the grass.
I dream of these thoughts for my heart's own romance,
and wish that certain lives would not have to pass.

Oh! poet of poets sing us another song,
may I see dead words come to life once again.
The crystal days are short, the nights are long,
my heart breeds emotions from your mystical pen.

Outside the rainy mist will begin to freeze,
dear William Butler how I wish you to be here.
As I wander to my bed and fall to my knees,
your words beneath my pillow whispering always in my ear.

State of being

The night was strung out like summer
waiting for school to start.
I was alone, waiting for the door
of the day to spring happily open.

The future always brings
expectations of grand experience
But there's nothing new, except
memories of yesterday.

People walk each day
waiting for the sun to set.

Maybe I expect too much,
Maybe I see too little,
Like the shore I am alone,
waiting for another wave.

If your wants are essential
to your needs—
If your reality cannot
exist without your dreams,
Then the two will reach
a bliss state of being.

Circles repeat

<pre>
                    The
          returning   world
       circle   out
        the   of
         in   night
       rhyme   waking.
    The   The
     burning   dawn
      rotation   in
        in   its
         sun   flight
              The breaking.
</pre>

Drunk on a sentimental breeze

Tingles of Chinese chimes
a song in the wind
visions of the land of lost
or to wherever things begin

Leaves twist to spindle
on stems of swaying trees
the sun sleeps on the horizon
pushed by a sensitive breeze

Past the skies of sorrow
into the orange of the sun
swept up to the land of never
to where all things have begun

Washed away by an angel's whisper
gone to the forgotten shore
where once i lay so tranquil
i dream i lie once more.

Dance with the angels

Flowers wilt with loneliness,
    love like the day falls,
        into the darkness,
        into the sadness,
           of the night.

Papers swirl within the wind,
    chills running crazy patterns down my back

My eyes stare,
    while my mind flows into the sadness of the spirit.

Walls close in,
    the sun loses herself to the mountains to the west,

Bright orange for a moment,
    then she rests,

Angels flutter their feathers around my world,
    red cheeked & happy as a smile

Loneliness has grabbed me by the teeth,
    not even the angels can free me from its cold corner

I must wait till she sleeps,
    then to slip between her lips,
and dance with the angels once again.

I was told

I was told not to write
in rhyme—
It wasn't cool—
It was like spilling mustard
on somebody's blue suede shoes—

I was told to make
my bed and
to bend down to
reach the sky—
I was told God
was dead, and that
was the answer to my question why?

I was told Hitler was a painter,
well what did he paint?
and if he was the anti-Christ
was Roosevelt the saint?

I was told of the floods
and the rising tides—
I was told of the hunger
that fills the belly of
the world.

I was told that I am
just the echo of the
first man who walked

I was told he screamed so loud
that in my dreams I can hear him,
but I can't make out what it is he says

Maybe it's a joyous cry from Lazarus
telling us
he's really not dead.

Maybe might come

maybe might come
but I doubt it.

it's always so unreliable
and anxious and obnoxious.

maybe might come
but it's never on time.

it's always someplace else
that's why it's never here.

maybe might come
but if it did

then it wouldn't be maybe,
it would be is, or now, or yes,

but it's not.
maybe just isn't;
yet.

They say you're gone

they say you're gone
but they got it all wrong.
I know you're here
I can still feel your
warm cheer.
Your Christian eyes
wave hello
I hear your voice
ring out
like a favorite bird;
and hear your words
amid the laughter
gone
no
never
always there when I
close my eyes
perfect souls
never die.

THE SEASONS

Winter-rest

Snow upon Country Graveyards,
So silent,
So quietly placid,
At rest,
   And in the State of Perfect Peace.

Spring

March is just beginning
soon however
she will shake the snow
off her branches and pass—
Spring will blossom
and laugh,
and smiles will be abundant—

A thunderstorm sweeping eastward

They're plowing the fields,
and it's Spring in front of my house.

Through the winter snow
she comes, and the sun blossoms.

The water from the streams rise
All things sleeping lift their eyes—
with day dispersing the final surprise,
a thunderstorm sweeping eastward.

September

Ice surrounding soul—
seeking something to do with time,
it slips through the crying cracks
of my days and frees itself.

On the road
I can wheel and deal,
be a real lazy,
crazy,
run-around youngster.

Taught doesn't learn you nothin',
learning teaches you the rotation
of the great wheel,
the one that turns the earth
moves the clouds,
makes tears roll down my cheeks.

Walking home

trees trembled
spooking the leaves

out of their branches.

thunder pounded
lightning
broke

rain fell like soldiers
in a field

    all at once

wiser creatures
were underground

i was walking home.

Winter

Winter slid in on her sled today,
with her cold fingers she cradled my face and I felt
a touch of warmth tingle my heart.
The children skate their youth away on a mirrored lake
that lies silent in a ghostly way—

Snowflakes are falling, another winter
to remember the chills of life, and the
silent lakes. The cold ground covers the dead,
warmth in their peace they can look at life,
and feel as silent as the lakes.

Request for forgiveness

August,
        hot and dusty,
the children exhausted and quick to rest feel the sun's
presence.
They accept the beads she has given them on their
young brows.

December,
        cold and cruel,
the children have but the emptiness of stomach and
stocking to be thankful for.
The wrongheaded winter has frozen both feet and heart.

May,
        For those and others,
it is long,
        the sea brings only future waves of sorrow and
frustration.

The dawn appears,
        there is but little light,
        and then there is dusk,
it brings only the moon and her shadow of sadness.
For all the dying lads,
For all the searching souls,
I feel the earth move with understanding and bow her
head in forgiveness,
        apologizing for her existence.

Never cold

The sun melts,
       each day the world spins,
Echoes of eternity,
       lovers pace beaches crying,
          crying,
               crying love.

With the faces of unknowns there is time to think,
       time for everything that must,
          & mustn't be done.

Falling off a star & landing in your arms.
The ice on the lake, soon to melt
Children soon to learn less about their existence,
       and more about others' existence,
Mountains drifting nowhere,
       living for a day,
          bye & bye
              no time to cry
              to live and die

Each day the night covers the stars,
With babies in Mother Nature's arms,
       they have no fears,
       no tears,
only the tragedy of growing old,
       but never cold.

She sits weather beaten,
        laughing like the wind,
knowing there is no place to go.

The world turns,
        The sun burns,
Babies flying from their nest into the circus,
Where everyone has their own original acts,
        Who is the audience?
Gliding, like a dying leaf to hit the ground
        and find relief.

Thoughts in winter gray

Sometimes in spring
The clover lies for miles on end
It runs through the fields
    like children

Blue skyline above
Sleeping on beds of green clover
Covered on top by blue blankets
Sweet thoughts in winter gray.

Snow gone rain

Snow gone rain now comes from the heavens,
lies on flower buds soon
to spring
in spring.

Snow gone rain canceling little league games,
leaving parks for lovers
under
umbrellas.

Snow gone rain painted clear on children's faces,
sneakers wet from
rain shower fun.

Snow gone rain drifting away on her clouds,
chasing snow forgotten skies
leaving us a rainbow.

Rain gone sun...

HUMAN BONDS

A dream from me to my family

The Irish mist soaks into my heart.
My blood tingles
on thoughts of being a poet.

Destiny will have her way,
        she always does.

My dream is of words to reflect my life.

My dream for my family is to see it smile
        beneath the sun.

 Ireland has given me her most precious gift,
        her words.

My family has given me her most precious gift,
        life worth while—

Grandma Mac

In your radiance
you have made the stars blush;
when the sun falls over
the shoulder of the world
I look for you.

Grandma
the winters are becoming colder;
we still cover the rose bushes
with autumn leaves—
Ireland is still at war,
Grandma are you warm?

Grandma
The river runs rapid
I'll meet you downstream—
Grandma
I love you
maybe I should have told you
more often.

To Mother

To you mother,
To kiss the feet of an angel would be yours.
I've seen your smile,
      and more so your tears.
I've grown in your arms and watched your beauty
      live with your life.
I want happiness to laugh alongside of you.
I want the children of your life to be your smile.
I want you to see me in the other world,
      and hold me in your arms once again.

To my family

My thoughts are uncontrollable,
as they seem to create tears,
           at times.
And I know I love you.
The family grows old and dusty,
           death lurks at each corner of our lives.
The clock on my wall smiles,
           it is patient.
I bless the fractional moment on earth that we
           have touched together.
If nothing more,
      you,
My family,
      have made me love.

Father

In the mirror of my life I see your face.
Sometimes it scares me for I know little
about the man it reflects.
But,
the sun stands at a distance,
to walk to her for self-fulfillment will be a journey.
I have time in my hands now.
like the sands on an ocean beach it
may slip through my sometimes uncertain fingers.
But I am not afraid,
for I carry you with me in my thoughts.

Mother

mother
the comatose opaque face
under
the oxygen mask
surrenders unwillingly.

the cold hands
chillingly content in limp position
grasp nothing no more.
arms swollen with sores
ravaged from diabetes and cancer,
dangle off the bed.

mother
i saw your lips tighten
your teeth grit
then you were dead.

Brendan

i just want him to be well,
happiness is so hard to
find.
and when u think
you've found it, that's
when you're most
often blind.
i just want him to be
himself because,
sincerity is so often
lost.
and i want him to
remain himself, no
matter what the cost.
i just want him to
be my beloved
because the sea below
has the sky above
and each son should
have a father to love
a mother to rest
his head.

For Jay

time.
a dream.
made up of sentences.
a wandering
    romance
    of situation
and circumstance—
disguised as a jewel.
empty
as everything is real
misplaced.

For Jennifer

i gave you my smile
to take with you
a passport,
a refuge,
a glade in the deluge
of holy places;
a rock,
a catacomb,
a friendly oasis.

i gave you my smile
to give away,
a calling card,
a currency,
a gesture of pay

i gave you my smile
to give to your boy,
a circle,
a tide
for us to everlastingly
enjoy,

i gave you my smile
and all of my dreams
the sunshine of
its power
the grace of
its gleam.

For Bill Ritch

where I come from
the ancient game was played
a citadel was built
each stone was laid
by a man named Ritch
his legend known
Sewanhaka Lacrosse
he etched in stone.

we took our place
with Manhasset and the rest
and we lay claim
that we were the best
and took the field
the way great warriors do
and believed that victories
were our due…

and now tonight
you honour me
but without this citadel
this award could never be
for I am just a chapter
in a greater anthology
of Hayes and Salerno
of Kaley and Moran

a history of lacrosse
its crozier so grand
its catgut and laces
sparkle with each strand.

from Syracuse to
the Mason-Dixon and
wherever lacrosse is
played in the land.

I gave my thanks tonight,
to this architect
the giant of a man;
Mr. Bill Ritch
lacrosse coach
Sewanhaka High School.

Presented at Coach Ritch's induction into the Long Island Lacrosse Hall of Fame, February 1992

He made me seem alive
(For Dad)

one early morning
in july
i took out his Christmas
poems
and cried.
i don't know why?
it wasn't as if
he died.
i had just spent
time with him
up on Cape Cod
and he made me
seem alive.
and i wanted to watch
him jig
as he always did.
he made me
seem alive.

For Bonnie

in case i age
and the strength and
the fear and the anger
that i wage is not
enough to excite you

in case i go
and the wind and
the leaves and the
sleet and the snow
don't blow

and the corn and
the squash and the
wheat don't sow,

and all things great
and small
weak and tall
don't grow.

in case i die
and the heart and
the breath and the
mind don't shine; and
the arms and the legs
and the eyes can't find.

and all things unimportant
seem suddenly sublime
then the end
is a bend in the road
that we'll never find
a death i will always defend
you from.

THE DARKNESS

Time to leave

I am alone, though surrounded by neighbors.
Like the day that granted me life, another shall
take it away. My body dangles, transparent as a
sun's ray that bursts into the young ladies' eyes.

With loneliness in my heart, and cold as my
companion, I wonder. Another day runs by my face
and I am still existing, as I contemplate my purpose.

The wind swirls snow beneath my still body,
as I try in desperation to hang on to life.

Spring will soon be born, for most it is a time
of happiness and reincarnation. But where there
is life there is death, and so be it.

Late March, with her warm overcoat covering
my body and buttoned to the top, she warns me it
is time to leave,...

Into nothingness my body drips. I am now
melting into the sullen mist of death, to reappear
some place else, some other time. Life has
ended for an icicle on a lonely winter-spring day.

The madman's song

The madman sits singing,
isolated in one of the corners of the universe.
There are so many corners you know?
His eyes penetrate past the real and abstract,
searching their way through the fog
of communication
trying in vain to uncover truth.

Communication is just another word,
the clock on the wall dies,
but not time.
Not even time can take communication
from its warm and waiting womb.

Nietzsche stared,
went mad,
knew truth and now sits in his corner.
Truth as thin as wind,
comes face to face within.
The fog horns are blowing across the truthless seas
of man,

They sing not of communication nor its birth.
But rather of truth,
they sing to the madman,
who hears them moaning, Godot is not coming.

One too many rides to rainbow lake

out in the streets
screams & laughter
brain bursting blues
of god and hereafter
cut the noose
loosen the laces
its cold white death
at a million paces

raindrops like thunder
tumble down slow
lost in the twilight
of crystal snow
cut the wrist
slit the throat
or just drink it down slow
raindrops like thunder
with no place to go

murder at morn
stabbed by the sun
roses have thorns
you're the one
cut it free
split out fast
it's the future you see
and the future's your past

on rainbow lake
where the water's calm
with venom in veins
and needle through arms
old timers remember
the wild cat's mistake
of one too many rides
to rainbow lake.

Little to nothing

The day drops
into evening's hands—
I rejoice—
I cannot help but feel
the weight of the seasons pressing me
between the months, weeks and days
of this existence.
I grow without the aid
of another beside me
and converse with loneliness—
We speak in two angled fork tongue—
We try, but fail to fool one another—
because there is little to nothing,
or nothing too little to say,
we talk in riddles and pass away—

Gray
(The colour of the day)

Walk with me,
    I am tired.

The sea comes up and drags me into the shallow waters
    of death.
My eyes see this world too clearly to see and think
    with empathy.
The hills are soft brown now, and death runs down my
    cold spine.

Pale snows sway down upon my untidy coat, and standing
in this lonesome nowhere, I have begun to weep.
I want to return back to the womb,
back from where I came,
maybe to start anew,
maybe never to return.

Sad hearts suckled by wolves, deep in the forest fortitude,
    safe for now.

Trees are naked, with their thin branches clutching to
one another they are secure. Flags of desperation hang
high on the pole. I see the sun from day to day and yet it
is the sky that mixes my emotions, for it is ever changing.

It is now forgotten gray,
it stands over me like six feet of topsoil,
walk with me,
        I am tired.

What do you look at on the I.R.T. 6?

Forget *The Times, The Post,*
The Daily News,
the stench from dry urine
at your shoes,
what do you look at
on the I.R.T. 6?

Forget the ads, the posters,
the subway map,
the meat-cleaver kid
with his psychotic attacks,
what do you look at
on the I.R.T. 6?

Forget the fag, the straight,
the youth-gang-punk,
the bag women, the monk,
what do you look at
on the I.R.T. 6?
what do you look at
on the I.R.T. 6?

Forget the cop, the nun,
the Krishna, the Moon,
the cad with the jive-ass,
the turkey, the goon,
what do you look at
on the I.R.T. 6?

Forget the psycho, the sicko,
the sucker, the saint,
forget the guys who've "got it"
and the guys who ain't,
what do you look at
on the I.R.T. 6?

Forget the broker, the doctor,
the nympho nurse,
the 20-minute delay
that makes it 10 times worse.
what do you look at
on the I.R.T. 6?
what do you look at
on the I.R.T. 6?

Does your mind turn pages
in a magazine?
do you read the articles
and know what they mean?
or do you just thumb through the pages,
go along with the scheme,
play out your role
in this Ionesco dream?

Rush home to dinner
and the evening news.

Dreaming

The Earth Covers My Father's Father
            And So On…
I Wonder How They Felt By Her Coldness
And Lack Of Character—

        It's A Circle Invisible
            Yet So Clear—
        It's Questions Unanswerable
            Or Perhaps Answered Unclear.

Mingling With Frustrated Periods
            Of Time.
Thomas Paine Where Are You Now The
S.L.A. Has Come And Gone Like A Lightning
Bolt, Leaving Her Shadow Of Hope Burning
With The Flesh Of Her Heroes.

        It's A Circle Invisible
            Yet So Clear—
        It's Questions Unanswerable
            Or Perhaps Answered Unclear.

The Capitalists Are Drinking Human
Blood From Their Golden Chalices.
They Swallow The Poor Man's Dreams
Leaving Him Crawling At The Steps
            Of Tomorrow.

Festival of darkness

The dime stores close,
the sun fades over the western fence.
Pedicabs stop,
nighttime with all illusions sprays the landscape.
Stars ill-mannered and ill-tempered quarrel aimlessly
       with a patch of clouds.

The new moon hangs herself with one of her rings.
Rime covers the fingers of the sweetbrier,
and the pathetic condition of midnight
drowns the festival of darkness,
       until the dawn.

Round & round

The sun stares into her eyes,
   she cries,
day's glory locks with night's fury,
they chase each other round & round,
   beginning,
       ending,
which is which,
   what's the difference?

Dogs bark,
   children weep,
doors closing with night left inside,
   Death waits patiently,
the old man with his baggy pants,
   and shaggy beard,
       laughs.

Mind drifts

Drifting into Raskolnikov's fields of melancholy.
My tear ducts are freezing
and the smiles of children are fading with each breath I take.
What is left?
Perhaps my winterized heart shall melt?
I have little left in my life to burn
except for letters never written and my sensitive skin.
Intonations of depression echo
through empty halls of my brain
and the smiling face can find tears falling from its cheeks.
I can no longer hide beneath the dark blanket
of a youthful night.
Visionary thoughts will not dissolve
and so their spirits lurk within my mind
like history's shadow upon the present.
Youth makes us carry flowers of universal colors
into the empty havens of hell.
And deity died when man was born.
Time will sleep in her death bed,
the moon shall be the mad sphere of the universe,
the sun shall ride her psychopathic path,
and man will drown in his seas of lifelessness,
then there shall be no more painful visionary thoughts—

Alone

With winter,
       With cold,
the shadow of the dead man lies fatal in all my dreams.
Sails slip slyly past the horizon into the unknown,
bringing nothing with it but the emptiness of death
And that winter snows that chilled sun & soul,
With the howls of strays,
       Lost & forgotten
Sing like the desert where nothing grows but nothingness
Eyes that have decayed,
       like the dreams of humanity sink & fall.
          always falling,
from the hands of helpless children.
This to be tragedy,
       or to be humor,
But always to be always,
       never to be changed.
I have no answer,
       nor seek to find.
They have been found,
       in a deserted valley of life,
       in the naked autumn trees, helpless, alone,

Always accepting winter,
       never to be changed.
With winter,
       With cold,

The shadow of the dead man lies fatal in all my dreams,
The mist is clearing,
          the fatal face soon to be seen.
When the shadow is uncovered it shall be my own.

It's raining

It's raining again,
it always does you know,
Birds fly for shelter,
dogs runnnnnnnnnnn
I am left in a puddle saturated in sadness.
The doorbell rings,
Chinese laundry lands upon my naked feet.
What a day!
What a devil's day!

Two eggs, some bacon, Sir Francis that is,
a shot of Jack D & I am off.
If I found that fellow that invented cities I'd throw
him a lollypop!

The streets run like a madman's brain only
confined by corners
Up to the top of crickety stairs,
and then it starts.

Louis, the secretary you hired then fired,
you can't do that—she quit.
A garbage man was bit by the janitor,
he's going to press charges.
Louis, are you hitting that bottle again?

Go have cookies & milk with the boss's daughter,
No, I better have a shot,
ONE more hour,
        then it's back to the street,
                back to those ugly walls,
                        another shot,
                                to sleep.
Waking up,
        it's raining,
                nothing new,
                        no, nothing new.

Once there were dreams

Under the willows of my mind
        she sits.
Captured Spring days and other bits
of memories lie beside her.
Once there were dreams of:
        houses,
        and children,
            love seats,
            and all.
Now there is but the remains
of an abandoned dream house filled
with empty hearts; and voices
        hollow & dry.

Under the willows of my mind;
        she lies;
quiet like an April night
that has been blown away.

Children holding hands dance
        around the willows;
A candle burns within my heart.
It flickers and twists and
then gently passes away;
        leaving behind only
      the darkness of loneliness.

Vietnam

The tree hangs like the death forgotten fields of war
Babies cry in the absence of their fathers
who have gone like the kind words of mankind.
Who did you expect would believe your satin tongues?
Wives weep asking for lovers to return,
still the houses burn,
I hear the guns of the imperialist rage
with God on their side.
I hear the bitter cold winds of war grow colder
across our country.
I hear the earth with all her voices laugh
while she swallows the dead.
I hear the name of Jesus used to protect
their guilty bodies from the action of genocide.
Flow with the stream of human wastes,
let your leaders be your guide,
When the war of guns is over,
you will lose the one inside.

Coney Island

down on the dirty streets
of coney island

where the snow turns black
before reaching the ground

where the litter blows in swirls
& people's fingers freeze
from not enough clothing

there are voices like sirens wailing.

out from the burnt black windows
of the drug-infested tenements
runs the yellow puss
of social sickness

down the dingy wall
it runs

down west 27th street
up to cropsey ave

across the roads
of people bleeding
another man's been stabbed.

in the gutter
a woman lies
burnt black holes
now her eyes

a scream from a window
a child cries
a round of fire
humanity dies.

coney island
they're selling 32 caliber pistols
to fifteen year olds
on your boardwalk

coney island
the garbage men hate to come

they say you're the worse thing
since harlem

shooting a boy in bayridge
throwing another in front of a train

stabbing a third under boardwalk lights
coney island you've gone insane.

coney island you're a hotdog
coney island land of rides

there's a sickness
growing out of you

& there's humans still inside.

coney island
your beach head is crying

the gulls are belly up

they said there'll be no more flying
they said they've had enough.

coney island
street gangs are taking over

anarchy like egg
on your face

coney island
they say when you don't feel
like a man in coney island

you feel like a fly in a bottle

coney island
your community lies frigid & fallow

coney island
there's a woman lying
in the middle of neptune ave

she's screaming kill me
cause it's getting cold
& I've got no place to go

kill me because the housing moratorium
has left me in the snow

coney island
u send your children
to riker's island
u pack them into jails

coney island
there must be something
that must be done

there must be a way
to heal your wounds

coney island
the train still runs to u

but no one wants to come

you're like an old person
making a lot of noise

they want to shut u down

they want u in your poverty
to be forever poverty bound

coney island
i love u
u saved my brother's life

the phoenix house on 31st st.
it cured his sickness
made him whole
gave him life again

coney island
I'm wishing the same for u.

I wish to be wind

Morning neatly tucks her shadow under her dress
to begin her routine day.

Snow
        falls from a sad sky and leaves her icy tears for us.
I became obsessed at youth to leave something behind.
Now I understand it will be my corpse
and a gravestone that reads,

Who was he that dared to take this plot of land?
Certainly forgotten bones, and not a man?

        Maybe a dream or two left within my coat pocket,
perhaps a picture of my life.

But nothing more,
        nothing less.
        To return to the ghost town,
finding time elapses
the clock on the wall collapses.
My world abandoned by sea and star
It's a dying dog's bark heard afar.

        Kicking an empty can across the road,
feeling the emptiness of its clang.
Bring me to my youth and let me off
        I've had enough.

I wish to be the wind,
perhaps create a storm.
Distort the fair system for an instant, then fall
into death's awaiting arms.

Two on a two-two train

"excuse me!
I was speaking to you…
I said, my train of thought
is stubborn…straight-
forward & goal oriented!
how 'bout yours?"

"my what?…oh,
I'm sorry…
mine's distant…winding…
derailed…
full of dizzy
straphangers…
strangling in
dream."

Lifeless

rolling tumbleweed of
dry thought...
where once a fountain
a flower,
a heart,
now
lifeless,
nothing,
a shapeless art,
a
void,
deep,
   mysterious,
            dark.

Madhattan

madhattan my friend roy
tells me you're an insane
asylum
turned inside out.
you're like a kid on the
corner
picking his nose.
wake the fuck up!
sometimes i'd like to kick
you right between your
twin towers.
rush, rush, rush,
that's all i ever get from
u,
where the fuck you goin'
anyway?
dressed in drag
lookin' like the big mama
that you are
where u going?
down to the
piers?
chasing the Chinese
new year?
slow down
take some advice

from the brothers
uptown,
let it all come to
u.

LOVE

Love song '74

She was
a flower in a field of fields,
      one to admire,
yet not love,
      one to hold,
yet not touch.
Can you give to one, your love?
No, better to create love,
      with time,
      with smiles,
      with tears.

She was
an angel that fell,
      but could not catch.
A woman at my doorstep,
      but could not greet.
Can you give to one, your love?
No, better to create love,
      with men,
      with thoughts,
      with words.
I will create the thought of love,
      for which I love.
And finding love in this,
I will have loved—

The search
(in the end finding nothing)

One little boy searched for love,
along the dusty trails of laughter and joy he traveled,
under deceptive stones he sorts,
through false meadows the winds blew,
still love like the timeless fugitive
lay hidden so well.

Behind her truth she sees all,
letting only deserving see her.
Her face transparent,
as light through dust particles in a forgotten cellar.
Her arms endless,
like her history that wraps around the human race.
Her body warm,
as the sun in summer coating a virgin's back.

Love,
you will not find her in want nor need,
for her angel feet may only be heard
tiptoeing across the sandy beaches of time
if we are silent,
and if we are giving,
not searching.

Wink

when u wink
i think
i'm going crazy
the way u move
excites the dead…
i'm quite ahead
of u in my love
it stretches
like a cloud
into all corners of
your sphere
and i'm here
whenever u need me
like a fiddle to
play
all u have to do
is wink.

Arguments

i'm an umpire,
i say,
"one more word and
you're out!"
as i drive you crazy
and you drive me wacko
down 244th street.
i drive you further
and you say that
extra word,
which drives me to
spin the car around
the corner,
taking you home
i say, "now get out!"
so you wipe your
face like home plate
and pout
slamming the door
crying
running to your house.

i roll down my window
and holler to you
just before you get
to your dugout

i say, "i'm sorry
baby you can be
up again."

this makes you smile
and your heart sings
and you come back up
hitting homeruns
over all my fences...

If she only knew

She had crazy hair
spilling down her back
and I dreamed of running
through it…
Oh! if only she knew
the magic in my heart
the magic of my dreams.

Sunlight

Sunlight breaks evenly
in the morning
and awakens all things.
Love like sunlight
breaks
evenly, and awakens.
Love like life
moving in circles.

Letter of love

Your letter was
a sweet renaissance—
a season of spring.
However,
I fear the winds bring winter,
and other sorrowful things.

For Cindy and Eddy
on marriage

They were young,
and had kissed each other's hearts.
The music was theirs,
now nothing could keep them apart.

Her hair was like snow blown strands
free and falling,
in the light of love
she answered his calling.

(To be poor or rich
and never care which.
For better or worse
love must come first.
To cry and to sing
and let marriage bring,
two people closer together.)

They are free
in their bondage
and glow in her light.
They are wings
of the dove,
rising in flight.

They are the grass
and the stars and
the white of the moon.
They are the love
that they weave,
with a friendship loom.

Shore girl

On the beach
the sun is setting
her hair
like wind blown strands
is whipping with each wave.

Free and lonely

I leave you at the bus station
waving farewell from behind a
stained glass window,
your eyes glow like children.

Having kissed,
emptiness settles in like bad weather
The sun splashes your face
as you ward it off with a protective squint.
The scars above your brow
mix with your frown;
thinking maybe you want to cry.
I cry inside.

Thoughts
are being forced
between my ears...
They batter down the east iron gates
that I have set strong before my heart.
(sorrow flowing
neither one knowing
where they're going)
(you want to be free,
I dream I want you
and you want to have me
and yet there's other things too!)

Down the road
the bus tumbleweeds away;
following each other's eyes
we feel dismay.
For though we wish each other
we need ourselves
and love for now
must rest on shelves
or farewell bus stations
where free hearts dwell.

Spring love

The day wakes up singing
with the arrival of spring birds—
In the distance
we leave winter behind
over the west hills
beyond the mountains
where the sun yawns—
collecting flowers barefoot
she smiles
spreading her love out
like a tablecloth
on a field of clover

You and me

You were from the mountains
and there you'll most likely stay—
learning new brilliance; knowing
the knowledge of the hills...
I shall be by the sea
for like your mountains
she teaches me wisdom,
and when we meet
in the foothills of thought
we will know the same things,
differently—

Friends and lovers

Friends as seasons
   come & go,
buried memories
beneath fallen snow.
Lightly after they fall
   meeting old & new
as they sway gently to perfection.
Can we ask what is it for?
Here & there & then no more!
Alas! there must be something
   to show
for all the pain & promises.

There she sits
   her eyes in love
melting my life with pleasant perception
   Hair
that spills to the shoulders
I speak of things of concern,
   she listens like the wind.

I laugh like the clouds
   she smiles like the sun
I cry like a stream
She catches me in her hands
   drinks & understands.

Strange café
(Somewhere south of my mind)

Outside the café
surrounded by spring fever
with flowers full bloom
   I sat.

She came with my meal
and whispered to be seated
No time for introduction
   she insisted

Do you taste loneliness between
the bread that you eat
or do your eyes of blue tell lies?
   she asked.

My bed lies cold
though be it spring
my flesh needs flesh
my blankets warmth
   I spoke.

Then throw on your cape
let us travel together through dark nights
you may have my inquisitive flesh
and I the blue from your eyes—

Time to find love

In a day,
       or a way,
She sings her songs,
Spring jumps up and catches all the flowers.
When the church bells ring the grass grows new
While I watch the angels smile.

In some love the world laughs,
But in all love there must be tears.
She smiles the smile I love,
       I hope my world is carried in her purse.

In the heart the emotions run,
       Time for tears,
          Time for fun,
Time to find love in a world where
       angels are always singing.

But ... love

still systematically
      we search for clues...
silently rubbing off the etchings on the walls
for things we cannot explain.

tell me what it is & I'll tell you what it's used for.
ask me the stations of the cross
& three times falls the enigma!
but of dust?

very little...no...nothing...
except what was...will be...
what never was...what will never be,
        but
            love—

Letter to an unknown love

(our lives are only dreams
a space in time
between the beams
of sunlight splashing
on winter streams)

My thoughts are like winds that whirl.
On psychic avenues they dance and swirl.
Slowly spindle, then finally curl,
    around you my love.

If you were only here where I could see,
to fall in love, you and me,
we'd rent a cottage on the other side
have a horse and a buggy and give free rides,
to children laughing before they cry,
before they age, before they die.
With braided hair covered in snow,
your eyes sparkle in the light of love's glow,
you turn to smile and I feel the relief
of the earth's soil and the sun's heat.

And then at night we could love and learn
to watch the skies twist and turn
and feel the stars, the universe burn,
    between our lips.

But now my love I bid farewell,
with a kiss to love and a curse as well.
For in the seasons spills the sand,
love & loved, and in the end faintly do I understand.

You

more and more and more I change
and without you
I could never hope to rearrange
the continual content
of what I ever hope to mean
and in the end
I am only what I seem
a constantly changing image
of what I dream,
one individual,
hopelessly
hopeless,
beyond his mean.
but with you, baby,

with you
i am,
i am always
i.

Kaleidoscopic mornings

she has white rooms &
in the mornings
in winter
the air conditioner
drowns the sounds
of city traffic
or so she says
shivering beneath blankets.

prisms
        spindle
in all her windows.
she has placed them there.
stars for her galaxy.
planets for her solar system.
toys
for her sun to burn through.
I wake
nude
in the crystal mornings
and catch the sun
warm, bright,
transcripting
kaleidoscopic transplanting colors
through lasers of light,
true contemporaries
in a gallery of white.

Alone

the phone rang
he wasn't home
in his living room
the music played
we sat alone...

the phone rang
he sipped his drink
the lights glowed
as he tried to think
alone...

the phone rang
he smoked his fag
through misfortune's zone
he did a neurotic-charleston-rag
alone...

the phone rang
love called across the wire
in a fat couch
clothed in apathy
and ill-desire
he sat alone...
no one to answer the phone.

Just a boy

i am just a boy
for you
and i don't ever want
to wear a feather
in my cap.

i like you like that,
when you smile
and you say
you are just my
boy,
a toy,
a great big boy
of fun,
for you to beat
like a drum into a
song.

It's true

as sad as it is
it is always like that,
no need to go on.
no mystery.
only pain.
and yet the poem is
euphoria.
for no matter how painful
it is,
it's true.
and the truth always hurts
and the truth always sets
you free.
so when a love leaves you
it's always painful;
and it's always true
and it's always free;
so as sad as it is;
go on.
because it hurts.
and it's true
and it's free—

Down by the ocean

i'm getting some
quid
together,
for a rainy
day,
i'll be down
by the
ocean.
i'll see u
now
by the briny
wave,
i'm feeling your
heart's
devotion.
what is it
now
that
i wish to
save?
i'll never know
the meaning...
be with me now,
oh my
beloved;
or can it
be
i'm dreaming—

AFTERWORD

Wherever I go
I won't go without you
for you'll always be in my heart,
And though years will pass
when I can't hold you close
we still will not be apart

You can rest in my dreams
when the evening is still
and the sunset quiets the day,
I'll listen for your heart
and remember—
you are not really away

Wherever I am
you'll be there with me
I promise I'll never let go
for love is a song
that once started, plays on...
and the music, both of us know

b. j. m.